soup plus

THE AUSTRALIAN
Women's Weekly

CONTENTS

AUSTRALIAN CUP AND SPOON MEASUREMENTS ARE METRIC. A CONVERSION CHART APPEARS ON PAGE 77.

Clear broths, creamy classics and hearty meal-in-a-bowl soups fill the pages of this very handy cookbook, perfect for those days you just crave the simplicity of a soup. We've also included accompaniments to turn simple into special; muffins, breads and crusty, cheesy toasts for your dipping pleasure.

Pamela Clark

Food Director

UDON AND PRAWN SOUP

prep + cook time 30 minutes **serves** 4
nutritional count per serving 1.5g total fat (0.3g saturated fat); 861kJ (206 cal); 16.2g carbohydrate; 30.3g protein; 2.3g fibre

3 cups (750ml) fish stock
3 cups (750ml) water
10cm stick fresh lemon grass (20g), chopped coarsely
4 fresh kaffir lime leaves, shredded finely
8cm piece fresh ginger (40g), sliced thinly
2 fresh small red thai chillies, chopped coarsely
1 tablespoon fish sauce
1kg uncooked medium king prawns
200g fresh udon noodles
230g can sliced bamboo shoots, rinsed, drained
100g fresh shiitake mushrooms, sliced thickly
60g baby spinach leaves

1 Combine stock, the water, lemon grass, lime leaves, ginger, chilli and sauce in large saucepan; bring to the boil. Reduce heat, simmer broth, uncovered, 10 minutes.
2 Meanwhile, shell and devein prawns, leaving tails attached.
3 Strain broth through sieve into large bowl; discard solids. Return broth to pan with prawns, noodles, bamboo shoots and mushrooms. Simmer, uncovered, about 5 minutes or until prawns are changed in colour and noodles are cooked as desired. Remove from heat; stir in spinach.

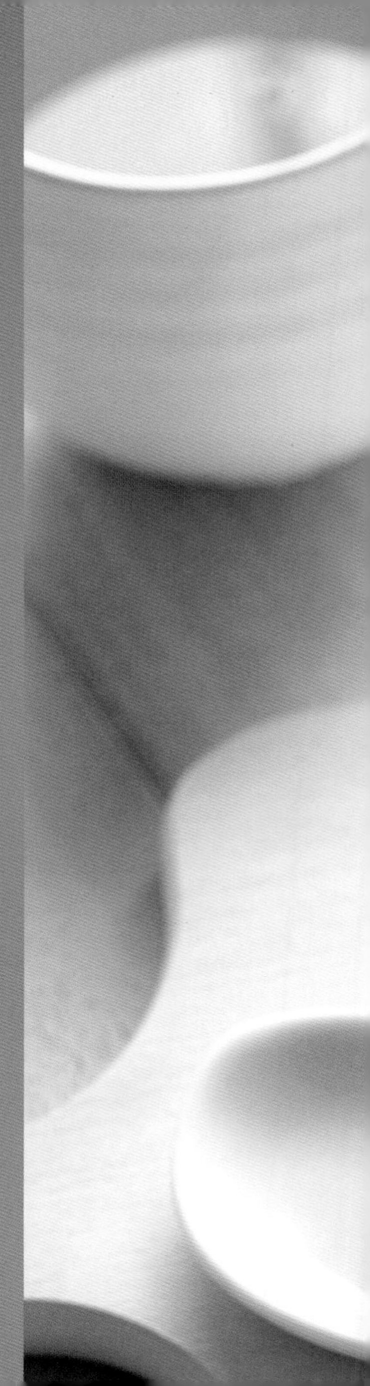

SOUPS

CREAM OF SPINACH SOUP WITH LEMON FETTA TOASTS

prep + cook time **55 minutes (+ cooling)** serves **6**
nutritional count per serving (incl. toasts)
25.8g total fat (16.2g saturated fat); 1676kJ (401 cal); 28.7g carbohydrate; 11.8g protein; 4.6g fibre

40g butter
1 large brown onion (200g), chopped finely
2 cloves garlic, crushed
3 medium potatoes (600g), chopped coarsely
3 cups (750ml) chicken stock
1 litre (4 cups) water
250g trimmed spinach, chopped coarsely
¾ cup (180ml) cream

1 Melt butter in large saucepan; cook onion and garlic, stirring, until onion softens. Add potato, stock and the water; bring to the boil. Reduce heat; simmer, covered, about 15 minutes or until potato is tender. Stir in spinach; stand soup 10 minutes.
2 Meanwhile, make lemon fetta toasts.
3 Blend or process soup, in batches, until smooth. Return soup to cleaned pan, add cream; stir over medium heat until hot.
4 Serve bowls of soup with toasts.
note **You need 1kg of untrimmed spinach to get the amount of trimmed spinach needed for this recipe.**

lemon fetta toasts
Preheat grill. Combine 150g fetta cheese with 1 teaspoon finely grated lemon rind. Cut 1 small french bread stick into 1.5cm slices; discard end pieces. Toast slices one side; turn, sprinkle each slice with fetta mixture and another teaspoon finely grated lemon rind. Grill toasts until heated through.

chicken, pea and asparagus soup with pistou

CHICKEN, PEA AND ASPARAGUS SOUP WITH PISTOU

prep + cook time **35 minutes** serves **4**
nutritional count per serving **5.7g total fat (1.3g saturated fat); 861kJ (206 cal); 7.3g carbohydrate; 28.9g protein; 4.4g fibre**

3 cups (750ml) chicken stock
3 cups (750ml) water
1 clove garlic, crushed
¼ teaspoon coarsely ground black pepper
400g chicken breast fillets
170g asparagus, trimmed, chopped coarsely
1½ cups (240g) shelled fresh peas
1 tablespoon lemon juice
pistou
½ cup coarsely chopped fresh flat-leaf parsley
½ cup coarsely chopped fresh mint
¼ cup coarsely chopped fresh garlic chives
2 teaspoons finely grated lemon rind
1 clove garlic, crushed
2 teaspoons olive oil

1 Bring stock, the water, garlic and pepper to the boil in large saucepan. Add chicken; return to the boil. Reduce heat; simmer, covered, about 10 minutes or until chicken is cooked through. Cool in poaching liquid 10 minutes. Remove chicken from pan; reserve poaching liquid. Slice chicken thinly.
2 Meanwhile, make pistou.
3 Add remaining ingredients to poaching liquid; bring to the boil. Return chicken to pan; simmer, uncovered, about 3 minutes or until vegetables are just tender.
4 Divide soup among serving bowls; top with pistou.
pistou Using mortar and pestle, pound ingredients until smooth.
note **You need 450g of fresh peas in the pod or 2 cups (240g) frozen peas for this recipe.**

thai chicken noodle broth

THAI CHICKEN NOODLE BROTH

prep + cook time **30 minutes** serves **4**
nutritional count per serving **7.1g total fat (2.2g saturated fat); 1208kJ (289 cal); 27.5g carbohydrate; 27.6g protein; 1.7g fibre**

1 litre (4 cups) chicken stock
2 cups (500ml) water
3cm piece fresh ginger (15g), grated
1 fresh small red thai chilli, chopped finely
400g chicken breast fillets, sliced thinly
400g fresh rice noodles
1 tablespoon fish sauce
1 tablespoon grated palm sugar
1 tablespoon lime juice
2 baby buk choy (300g), quartered
⅓ cup loosely packed thai basil leaves

1 Combine stock, the water, ginger and chilli in large saucepan; cover, bring to the boil. Reduce heat; simmer 5 minutes. Add chicken, noodles, sauce, sugar and juice; simmer about 5 minutes or until chicken is cooked through and noodles are tender.
2 Divide buk choy among serving bowls; ladle chicken broth into bowls. Sprinkle with basil.

SCOTCH BROTH WITH CHEESE SCONES

prep + cook time **2 hours 15 minutes** serves **4**
nutritional count per serving (incl. scones)
32.2g total fat (15.5g saturated fat); 3181kJ (761 cal); 59g carbohydrate; 52.8g protein; 12g fibre

2.25 litres (9 cups) water
1kg lamb neck chops
¾ cup (150g) pearl barley
1 large brown onion (200g), cut into 1cm pieces
2 medium carrots (240g), cut into 1cm pieces
1 medium leek (350g), sliced thinly
2 cups (160g) finely shredded cabbage
½ cup (60g) frozen peas
2 tablespoons coarsely chopped fresh flat-leaf parsley

1 Place the water in large saucepan with lamb and barley; bring to the boil. Reduce heat; simmer, covered, 1 hour, skimming fat from surface occasionally. Add onion, carrot and leek; simmer, covered, about 30 minutes or until carrot is tender.
2 Meanwhile, make cheese scones.
3 Remove lamb from pan. When cool enough to handle, remove and discard bones; shred lamb coarsely.
4 Return lamb to soup with cabbage and peas; cook, uncovered, about 10 minutes or until cabbage is just tender.
5 Serve bowls of soup sprinkled with parsley; accompany with scones.

cheese scones

Preheat oven to 220°C/200°C fan-forced. Grease and flour 8cm x 26cm bar pan. Combine 1 cup self-raising flour, a pinch of cayenne pepper, 2 tablespoons finely grated parmesan cheese and ¼ cup coarsely grated cheddar cheese in medium bowl; pour in ½ cup milk, stir until mixture forms a sticky dough. Gently knead dough on floured surface until smooth; flatten dough to 2cm-thickness. Using 4.5cm cutter, cut rounds from dough; place rounds, slightly touching, in pan. Brush scones with a little milk then sprinkle with ¼ cup coarsely grated cheddar cheese. Bake about 20 minutes.

tomato and fennel soup with croûtons

TOMATO AND FENNEL SOUP WITH CROUTONS

prep + cook time **1 hour** serves **4**
nutritional count per serving **4.3g total fat (0.8g saturated fat); 589kJ (141 cal); 17.3g carbohydrate; 7.5g protein; 5.9g fibre**

2 teaspoons olive oil
1 medium fennel bulb (300g), chopped coarsely
2 medium brown onions (300g), chopped coarsely
2 cloves garlic, quartered
1kg tomatoes, quartered
3 cups (750ml) vegetable stock
4 slices (180g) white bread, crusts removed
cooking-oil spray

1 Preheat oven to 180°C/160°C fan-forced.
2 Heat oil in large saucepan; cook fennel, onion and garlic, stirring, until onion softens. Add tomato and stock; bring to the boil. Reduce heat; simmer, covered, stirring occasionally, 15 minutes. Uncover; simmer, stirring occasionally, about 15 minutes or until tomato is soft and pulpy. Stand soup 10 minutes.
3 Meanwhile, cut bread into 2cm cubes. Place on oven tray; spray lightly with oil. Toast, in oven, about 10 minutes or until croûtons are crisp.
4 Blend or process soup, in batches, until smooth. Pass soup through food mill or fine sieve; reheat soup in pan. Serve soup topped with croûtons.

BEEF AND BARLEY SOUP

prep + cook time **2 hours 15 minutes** serves **6**
nutritional count per serving **8.8g total fat (2.6g saturated fat); 1350kJ (323 cal); 30g carbohydrate; 26.9g protein; 7.8g fibre**

1 tablespoon olive oil
500g gravy beef, trimmed, cut into 2cm pieces
2 cloves garlic, crushed
2 medium brown onions (300g), chopped finely
¾ cup (150g) pearl barley
3 cups (750ml) beef stock
1.5 litres (6 cups) water
1 dried bay leaf

beef and barley soup

1 sprig fresh rosemary
1 sprig fresh thyme
2 medium potatoes (400g), cut into 1cm pieces
2 medium carrots (240g), cut into 1cm pieces
2 medium zucchini (240g), cut into 1cm pieces
2 medium yellow patty-pan squash (60g), cut into 1cm pieces
100g swiss brown mushrooms, chopped coarsely
½ cup finely chopped fresh flat-leaf parsley

1 Heat half the oil in large saucepan; cook beef, in batches, until browned. Remove from pan.
2 Heat remaining oil in same pan; cook garlic and onion, stirring, until onion softens. Return beef to pan with barley, stock, the water, bay leaf, rosemary and thyme, bring to the boil. Reduce heat; simmer, covered, 1 hour or until beef and barley are tender, skimming fat occasionally.
3 Add potato, carrot, zucchini, squash and mushrooms to soup; simmer, covered, about 25 minutes or until vegetables are softened. Remove and discard bay leaf, rosemary and thyme.
4 Serve bowls of soup sprinkled with parsley.

chicken chowder

CHICKEN CHOWDER

prep + cook time **55 minutes** serves **4**
nutritional count per serving **37.3g total fat (22.6g saturated fat); 2721kJ (651 cal); 36.1g carbohydrate; 41.7g protein; 4.6g fibre**

2 cups (500ml) chicken stock
2 cups (500ml) water
2 chicken breast fillets (400g)
40g butter
2 rindless bacon slices (130g), chopped coarsely
1 medium brown onion (150g), chopped finely
1 clove garlic, crushed
1 medium leek (350g), sliced thinly
1 stalk celery (150g), trimmed, chopped finely
¼ cup (35g) plain flour
2 medium potatoes (400g), chopped coarsely
1 litre (4 cups) milk
½ cup (125ml) cream
2 tablespoons finely chopped fresh chives

1 Bring stock and the water to the boil in medium saucepan; add chicken, return to the boil. Reduce heat; simmer, covered, about 10 minutes or until chicken is cooked through. Cool chicken in poaching liquid 10 minutes. Remove chicken from pan; discard poaching liquid. Shred chicken coarsely.
2 Meanwhile, heat butter in large saucepan; cook bacon, onion, garlic, leek and celery, stirring, until vegetables soften.
3 Stir in flour; cook, stirring, 1 minute. Stir in potato, milk and cream; simmer, covered, about 15 minutes or until potato is just tender.
4 Add chicken and chives; cook, stirring, until heated through.

BEEFY BLACK-EYED BEAN AND SPINACH SOUP

prep + cook time **2 hours 10 minutes (+ standing)**
serves **4**
nutritional count per serving **13.9g total fat (4.2g saturated fat); 2199kJ (526 cal); 28.3g carbohydrate; 62.6g protein; 12.4g fibre**

1 cup (200g) black-eyed beans
1 tablespoon olive oil
1 medium brown onion (150g), chopped finely
1 clove garlic, crushed
2.5 litres beef stock (10 cups)
¼ cup (60ml) dry red wine
2 tablespoons tomato paste
500g piece beef skirt steak
250g trimmed spinach, chopped coarsely

1 Place beans in medium bowl, cover with water; stand overnight, drain. Rinse under cold water; drain.
2 Heat oil in large saucepan; cook onion and garlic, stirring, until onion softens. Add stock, wine, paste and beef to pan; bring to the boil. Reduce heat; simmer, covered, 40 minutes. Uncover; simmer 30 minutes.
3 Remove beef from pan. Add beans to pan; bring to the boil. Reduce heat; simmer, uncovered, until beans are tender.
4 Meanwhile, when beef is cool enough to handle, remove and discard fat and sinew. Chop beef coarsely; return to pan with spinach; simmer, uncovered, until soup is hot.
note **You need 1kg of untrimmed spinach to get the amount of trimmed spinach required for this recipe.**

beefy black-eyed bean and spinach soup

BEAN AND MERGUEZ SOUP WITH GREMOLATA

prep + cook time **50 minutes** serves **4**
nutritional count per serving **42.4g total fat (15.6g saturated fat); 2504kJ (599 cal); 14.6g carbohydrate; 38.4g protein; 5.5g fibre**

1 medium red onion (170g), chopped coarsely
2 rindless bacon slices (130g), chopped coarsely
2 cloves garlic, crushed
400g can diced tomatoes
1.5 litres (6 cups) chicken stock
6 merguez sausages (480g)
2 x 400g cans white beans, rinsed, drained

gremolata

⅓ cup finely chopped fresh flat-leaf parsley
2 teaspoons finely grated lemon rind
2 cloves garlic, crushed

1 Cook onion, bacon and garlic in heated oiled large saucepan, stirring, until onion is soft and bacon crisp. Add undrained tomatoes and stock; bring to the boil. Reduce heat; simmer, uncovered, 20 minutes, stirring occasionally.
2 Meanwhile, cook sausages in heated oiled medium frying pan until browned and cooked through; slice thinly.
3 Make gremolata.
4 Add sausage to soup with beans; stir until soup is hot.
5 Serve bowls of soup topped with gremolata.
gremolata Combine ingredients in small bowl.

note **Merguez, the French spelling of the Arabic "mirqaz", is a small spicy lamb sausage available from many butchers, delicatessens and specialty sausage stores.**

mushroom soup with goat cheese croûtes

MUSHROOM SOUP WITH GOAT CHEESE CROUTES

prep + cook time **1 hour 10 minutes** serves **6**
nutritional count per serving **32.5g total fat (19.6g saturated fat); 1956kJ (468 cal); 25.5g carbohydrate; 15.7g protein; 7g fibre**

125g butter
400g button mushrooms, sliced thinly
300g medium cap mushrooms, sliced thinly
300g swiss brown mushrooms, sliced thinly
3 medium brown onions (450g), sliced thinly
2 cloves garlic, crushed
⅓ cup (50g) plain flour
2 cups (500ml) chicken stock
1.5 litres (6 cups) water
½ cup (120g) sour cream
2 teaspoons olive oil
100g enoki mushrooms
1 small french bread stick, cut into 12 slices
150g log goat cheese

1 Melt 50g of the butter in large saucepan; add button, cap and swiss brown mushrooms; cook, stirring, until softened. Remove from pan.
2 Heat remaining butter in same pan. Add onion and garlic; cook, stirring, until onion is soft. Add flour, stir 1 minute. Stir in stock and the water; return half of the cooked mushrooms to pan. Bring to the boil; simmer, uncovered, 30 minutes. Stand soup 10 minutes.
3 Blend soup, in batches, until smooth. Return to pan; whisk in sour cream and remaining cooked mushrooms. Bring to the boil; remove from heat.
4 Heat oil in small frying pan; cook enoki mushrooms over high heat until browned lightly.
5 Meanwhile, toast bread slices under hot grill until browned lightly; turn, spread with goat cheese, grill until cheese is heated.
6 Divide soup among serving bowls, top with enoki mushrooms; serve with croûtes.

CURRY AND LIME LENTIL SOUP

prep + cook time **45 minutes** serves **4**
nutritional count per serving **6g total fat (0.9g saturated fat); 991kJ (237 cal); 25.2g carbohydrate; 15.4g protein; 9.9g fibre**

2 teaspoons vegetable oil
1 tablespoon hot curry paste
1 medium brown onion (150g), chopped finely
2 cloves garlic, crushed
2cm piece fresh ginger (10g), grated
1 teaspoon cumin seeds
1 cup (200g) red lentils
2 cups (500ml) vegetable stock
2½ cups (625ml) water
400g can diced tomatoes
1 teaspoon finely grated lime rind
¼ cup (60ml) lime juice
⅓ cup chopped fresh flat-leaf parsley

1 Heat oil in large saucepan; cook curry paste, stirring, until fragrant. Add onion, garlic, ginger and cumin; cook, stirring, until onion softens.
2 Add lentils, stock, the water and undrained tomatoes; bring to the boil. Simmer, uncovered, about 20 minutes or until lentils are softened.
3 Stir in rind and juice; return to the boil. Remove from heat; stir in parsley.

curry and lime lentil soup

CAULIFLOWER SOUP WITH CHEESE AND BACON TOASTS

prep + cook time **40 minutes** serves **6**
nutritional count per serving (incl. toasts)
14.3g total fat (6g saturated fat); 1404kJ (336 cal); 33.1g carbohydrate; 18.5g protein; 5.3g fibre

1 tablespoon olive oil
1 medium brown onion (150g), chopped coarsely
2 cloves garlic, crushed
1 large potato (300g), chopped finely
1kg cauliflower, trimmed, chopped coarsely
3 cups (750ml) salt-reduced chicken stock
3 cups (750ml) water
2 tablespoons coarsely chopped fresh chives

1 Heat oil in large saucepan; cook onion and garlic over low heat, stirring, until soft but not coloured.
2 Add potato, cauliflower, stock and the water; bring to the boil. Reduce heat; simmer, covered, about 15 minutes or until vegetables are very soft. Stand soup 10 minutes.
3 Meanwhile, make cheese and bacon toasts.
4 Blend or process cauliflower mixture, in batches, until smooth; return to pan, stir gently over low heat until hot.
5 Divide soup among serving bowls; sprinkle with chives. Serve with cheese and bacon toasts.

cheese and bacon toasts
Preheat grill. Cut 3 thin rindless bacon slices into quarters; place on foil-covered oven tray and grill until crisp. Thinly slice 1 ciabatta bread loaf diagonally into 12 slices. Grill bread slices until browned lightly. Spread 1 tablespoon wholegrain mustard over bread slices. Divide 120g thinly sliced cheddar cheese evenly over slices; grill until cheese melts then top with bacon.

coconut and lemon grass pork and mushroom soup

COCONUT AND LEMON GRASS PORK AND MUSHROOM SOUP

prep + cook time **30 minutes** serves **4**
nutritional count per serving **19.2g total fat (14.4g saturated fat); 1517kJ (363 cal); 5.8g carbohydrate; 39.9g protein; 5g fibre**

1 litre (4 cups) chicken stock
2 x 140ml cans coconut milk
10cm stick fresh lemon grass (20g), chopped finely
5cm piece fresh ginger (25g), chopped finely
1 clove garlic, crushed
2 teaspoons fish sauce
600g pork fillets, sliced thinly
300g oyster mushrooms, halved
2 fresh long red chillies, sliced thinly
1 tablespoon lime juice
4 green onions, sliced thinly

1 Combine stock, coconut milk, lemon grass, ginger, garlic and sauce in large saucepan; bring to the boil. Reduce heat; simmer, covered, 10 minutes.
2 Add pork, mushrooms, chilli and juice; return to the boil. Reduce heat; simmer, covered, until pork is cooked. Serve sprinkled with onion.

LAMB SHANK SOUP

prep + cook time **3 hours 30 minutes (+ standing & refrigeration)** serves **4**
nutritional count per serving **28.2g total fat (9.9g saturated fat); 2654kJ (635 cal); 35.7g carbohydrate; 59.1g protein; 15.6g fibre**

1½ cups (300g) dried chickpeas
1 tablespoon olive oil
1.5kg lamb shanks
1 medium brown onion (150g), chopped finely
2 medium carrots (240g), chopped finely
2 stalks celery (200g), trimmed, sliced thinly
2 cloves garlic, crushed
1 teaspoon ground cumin
2 cups (500ml) chicken stock
1 litre (4 cups) water
8 large stalks silver beet (400g), chopped finely
¼ cup (60ml) lemon juice

1 Place chickpeas in medium bowl, cover with water; stand overnight. Rinse under cold water; drain.
2 Meanwhile, heat oil in large saucepan; cook lamb, in batches, until browned. Remove from pan. Cook onion, carrot, celery, garlic and cumin in same pan, stirring, about 5 minutes or until onion softens. Return lamb to pan with stock and the water; bring to the boil. Reduce heat; simmer, covered, 2 hours.
3 Remove soup mixture from heat; when lamb is cool enough to handle, remove meat, chop coarsely. Refrigerate cooled soup mixture and lamb meat, covered separately, overnight.
4 Discard fat from surface of soup mixture. Place soup mixture, meat and chickpeas in large saucepan; bring to the boil. Reduce heat; simmer, covered, 30 minutes. Add silver beet and lemon; simmer, uncovered, until silver beet just wilts.
serve with **warmed loaf of ciabatta.**

lamb shank soup

pea and ham soup with risoni

PEA AND HAM SOUP WITH RISONI

prep + cook time **1 hour 30 minutes** serves **6**
nutritional count per serving **3g total fat (0.6g saturated fat); 811kJ (194 cal); 30g carbohydrate; 9g protein; 4.6g fibre**

2 teaspoons olive oil
1 medium brown onion (150g), chopped
2 teaspoons ground cumin
2.5 litres (10 cups) water
2 stalks celery (300g), trimmed, chopped
2 dried bay leaves
1.5kg ham bone
1 cup (220g) risoni pasta
2 cups (240g) frozen peas
2 tablespoons finely chopped fresh mint

1 Heat oil in large saucepan; cook onion, stirring, until softened. Add cumin; cook, stirring, until fragrant. Add the water, celery, bay leaves and bone; bring to the boil. Reduce heat; simmer, covered, 1 hour, skimming occasionally.
2 Remove bone; when cool enough to handle, cut ham from bone, discarding any skin and fat. Shred ham finely.
3 Return soup to the boil; stir in ham, pasta and peas. Cook, uncovered, 5 minutes or until pasta is tender. Sprinkle bowls of soup with mint.

CREAMY TOMATO AND VEAL SOUP

prep + cook time **2 hours 30 minutes (+ cooling)** serves **6**
nutritional count per serving (incl. toast) **28.2g total fat (16.7g saturated fat); 2094kJ (501 cal); 33g carbohydrate; 26.3g protein; 5.4g fibre**

1 litre (4 cups) water
500g piece boneless veal shoulder
6 black peppercorns
1 dried bay leaf
60g butter
1 medium brown onion (150g), chopped
1 clove garlic, crushed
⅓ cup (50g) plain flour
6 large egg tomatoes (540g), chopped coarsely
2 tablespoons tomato paste
½ cup (125ml) cream
⅓ cup (75g) semi-dried tomatoes, drained, chopped finely
2 tablespoons finely shredded fresh basil

creamy tomato and veal soup

1 Place the water in large saucepan with veal, peppercorns and bay leaf; bring to the boil. Reduce heat; simmer, covered, about 1½ hours or until veal is tender.
2 Transfer veal to medium bowl; using two forks, shred veal coarsely. Strain broth through muslin-lined sieve or colander into large heatproof bowl; discard solids.
3 Melt butter in large saucepan; cook onion and garlic, stirring, until onion softens. Add flour; cook, stirring, until mixture thickens and bubbles. Gradually stir in broth; stir over medium heat until soup boils and thickens slightly. Add egg tomato and paste; return to the boil. Simmer, covered, 10 minutes. Cool 15 minutes.
4 Meanwhile, make toasted ciabatta with basil butter.
5 Blend or process soup, in batches, until smooth. Return soup to cleaned pan, add cream; stir over medium heat until hot.
6 Serve bowls of soup topped with shredded veal and semi-dried tomato, sprinkled with basil and accompanied with toasted ciabatta.

toasted ciabatta and basil butter
Combine 50g softened butter with 1 tablespoon finely chopped basil in small bowl. Toast 8 thick slices ciabatta bread; spread with butter.

ROASTED CAPSICUM SOUP WITH FRIED PROVOLONE POLENTA

prep + cook time **1 hour 30 minutes (+ refrigeration)**
serves **6**
nutritional count per serving (incl. polenta)
21.6g total fat (12g saturated fat); 1480kJ (354 cal); 27.3g carbohydrate; 11.6g protein; 3.4g fibre

4 medium red capsicums (800g)
2 cloves garlic, unpeeled
1 tablespoon olive oil
1 medium brown onion (150g), chopped finely
1 teaspoon sweet paprika
3 cups (750ml) water
1 litre (4 cups) chicken stock
½ cup (125ml) cream
2 teaspoons white sugar
1 tablespoon finely chopped fresh chives

1 Three hours before, make provolone polenta.
2 Quarter capsicums, discard seeds and membranes. Roast capsicum and garlic under grill or in very hot oven, skin-side up, until skin blisters and blackens. Cover capsicum pieces in plastic or paper for 5 minutes; peel away skin. Peel garlic; chop coarsely.
3 Heat oil in large saucepan; cook onion, stirring, until softened. Add paprika; cook, stirring, until fragrant. Add the water, stock, capsicum and garlic; bring to the boil. Reduce heat; simmer, uncovered, 40 minutes. Stand soup 10 minutes.
4 Meanwhile, turn polenta onto board, trim edges; cut in half lengthways, cut each half into 9 finger-sized slices. Cook polenta, in batches, in heated oiled large frying pan until browned both sides.
5 Blend or process soup, in batches, until smooth; return to cleaned pan. Add cream and sugar; stir over medium heat until hot.
6 Serve bowls of soup sprinkled with chives; accompany with fried provolone polenta.

provolone polenta
Oil 20cm x 30cm rectangular slice pan; line base and two long sides with baking paper, extending paper 5cm over long sides. Bring 3½ cups of water to the boil in medium saucepan. Gradually add 1 cup polenta, stirring constantly. Reduce heat; simmer, stirring, about 10 minutes or until polenta thickens. Stir in 20g butter and 1 cup coarsely grated provolone cheese. Spread polenta into pan, cover; refrigerate about 3 hours or until firm.

MINESTRONE

prep + cook time **1 hour 15 minutes** serves **6**
nutritional count per serving **6.2g total fat (2.7g saturated fat); 949kJ (227 cal); 29.7g carbohydrate; 12.7g protein; 7g fibre**

2 teaspoons olive oil
1 medium brown onion (150g), chopped finely
2 cloves garlic, crushed
1 stalk celery (150g), trimmed, chopped coarsely
1 large carrot (180g), chopped coarsely
1 litre (4 cups) vegetable stock
1 cup (250ml) water
800g can crushed tomatoes
1 medium zucchini (120g), chopped coarsely
2 cups (160g) finely shredded cabbage
150g small shell pasta
300g can white beans, rinsed, drained
¼ cup coarsely chopped fresh flat-leaf parsley
¾ cup (60g) shaved parmesan cheese

1 Heat oil in large saucepan; cook onion and garlic, stirring, until onion softens. Add celery and carrot; cook, stirring, 5 minutes.
2 Stir in stock, the water and undrained tomatoes; bring to the boil. Reduce heat; simmer, covered, about 20 minutes or until vegetables are tender.
3 Add zucchini, cabbage, pasta and beans; cook, uncovered, about 15 minutes or until pasta is tender. Stir in parsley.
4 Serve soup topped with cheese.

CREAM OF KUMARA SOUP WITH ROSEMARY SOURDOUGH

prep + cook time **40 minutes (+ cooling)** serves **6**
nutritional count per serving (incl. sourdough) **21.3g total fat (7.7g saturated fat); 2282kJ (546 cal); 70.9g carbohydrate; 13.2g protein; 8.8g fibre**

1 tablespoon olive oil
2 medium kumara (800g), chopped coarsely
1 medium brown onion (150g), chopped coarsely
2 cloves garlic, quartered
2 teaspoons coarsely chopped fresh rosemary

cream of kumara soup with rosemary sourdough

1 teaspoon finely grated lemon rind
2 cups (500ml) vegetable stock
2 cups (500ml) water
1 tablespoon lemon juice
½ cup (125ml) cream

1 Heat oil in large frying pan; cook kumara, onion and garlic, stirring, 10 minutes. Add rosemary, rind, stock and the water; bring to the boil. Reduce heat; simmer, covered, about 15 minutes or until kumara is soft. Stand soup 10 minutes.
2 Meanwhile, make rosemary sourdough.
3 Blend or process soup, in batches, until smooth. Return soup to cleaned pan, add juice; stir over medium heat until hot.
4 Serve bowls of soup drizzled with cream, accompanied with sourdough.

rosemary sourdough

Preheat oven to 180°C/160°C fan-forced. Cut 1 loaf sourdough bread into 3cm slices. Combine 2 tablespoons olive oil and 2 teaspoons finely chopped fresh rosemary in large bowl; add bread, turn to coat in mixture. Place bread on oven tray; toast bread, both sides, about 15 minutes.

HARIRA

prep + cook time **2 hours 40 minutes (+ standing)**
serves **8**
nutritional count per serving **8.6g total fat (4g saturated fat); 1095kJ (262 cal); 23.6g carbohydrate; 20.1g protein; 4.8g fibre**

1 cup (200g) dried chickpeas
20g butter
2 medium brown onions (300g), chopped finely
2 stalks celery (300g), trimmed, chopped finely
2 cloves garlic, crushed
4cm piece fresh ginger (20g), grated
1 teaspoon ground cinnamon
½ teaspoon ground black pepper
pinch saffron threads
500g diced lamb
3 large tomatoes (660g), seeded, chopped coarsely
2 litres (8 cups) hot water
½ cup (100g) brown lentils
2 tablespoons plain flour
½ cup (100g) cooked white long-grain rice
½ cup firmly packed fresh coriander leaves
2 tablespoons lemon juice

1 Place chickpeas in medium bowl, cover with water; stand overnight, drain. Rinse under cold water; drain.
2 Melt butter in large saucepan; cook onion, celery and garlic, stirring, until onion softens. Add ginger, cinnamon, pepper and saffron; cook, stirring, about 2 minutes or until fragrant. Add lamb; cook, stirring, about 5 minutes or until lamb is browned.
3 Add chickpeas and tomato; cook, stirring, about 5 minutes or until tomato softens.
4 Stir the water into the soup mixture; bring to the boil. Reduce heat; simmer, covered, 45 minutes. Add lentils; simmer, covered, 1 hour.
5 Blend flour with ½ cup of the slightly cooled broth in small bowl; return to pan with rice. Cook, stirring, until soup comes to the boil and thickens slightly. Remove from heat; stir in coriander and juice.

minted broad bean and ham soup

MINTED BROAD BEAN AND HAM SOUP

prep + cook time **3 hours** serves **4**
nutritional count per serving **7.4g total fat (2g saturated fat); 890kJ (213 cal); 13.4g carbohydrate; 17.7g protein; 11.4g fibre**

2 teaspoons olive oil
1 large brown onion (200g), chopped coarsely
2 stalks celery (300g), trimmed, chopped coarsely
1 medium carrot (120g), chopped coarsely
2 cloves garlic, crushed
1kg ham hock
2 litres (8 cups) water
3 cups (450g) frozen broad beans, peeled
1 tablespoon lemon juice
⅓ cup finely chopped fresh mint

1 Heat oil in large saucepan; cook onion, celery, carrot and garlic, stirring, until vegetables soften. Add ham hock and the water; bring to the boil. Reduce heat; simmer, covered, 1½ hours. Uncover; simmer 30 minutes.
2 Remove ham hock from soup; when cool enough to handle, remove meat from bone, shred coarsely. Discard skin and bone.
3 Meanwhile, add beans to soup; simmer, uncovered, 5 minutes or until beans are tender. Cool 5 minutes.
4 Using hand-held blender, puree soup, in pan, until soup is almost smooth. Return ham meat to soup with juice; cook, stirring, until hot. Serve soup sprinkled with mint.

HEARTY WINTER SOUP

prep + cook time **2 hours 25 minutes** serves **4**
nutritional count per serving **21.4g total fat (6.5g saturated fat); 2387kJ (571 cal); 22g carbohydrate; 58.5g protein; 7.6g fibre**

2 tablespoons olive oil
1kg gravy beef, trimmed, cut into 2cm pieces
12 shallots (300g), halved
2 cloves garlic, crushed
2 small parsnips (240g), chopped coarsely
2 small turnips (300g), chopped coarsely

hearty winter soup

2 medium swedes (450g), chopped coarsely
300g piece pumpkin, chopped coarsely
1 cup (250ml) dry white wine
3 cups (750ml) beef stock
3 cups (750ml) water
1 tablespoon tomato paste
4 sprigs fresh thyme
⅓ cup short-cut vermicelli noodles

1 Heat half the oil in large saucepan; cook beef, in batches, until browned. Remove from pan.
2 Heat remaining oil in same pan; cook shallots and garlic, stirring, until shallots soften.
3 Add vegetables, wine, stock, the water, paste and thyme; bring to the boil. Reduce heat; simmer, covered, 1½ hours, stirring occasionally.
4 Add noodles; cook, uncovered, 10 minutes or until just softened.

chicken and mushroom soup

CHICKEN AND MUSHROOM SOUP

prep + cook time **55 minutes** serves **4**
nutritional count per serving **37.1g total fat (13.3g saturated fat); 2140kJ (512 cal); 11.7g carbohydrate; 31.9g protein; 4.2g fibre**

¼ cup (60ml) olive oil
400g chicken breast fillets, chopped coarsely
3 green onions, sliced thinly
3 cloves garlic, crushed
300g button mushrooms, sliced thinly
3 cups (750ml) chicken stock
2 cups (500ml) water
100g cauliflower, chopped coarsely
2 small potatoes (240g), chopped coarsely
½ cup (125ml) cream
¼ cup (65g) basil pesto
1 tablespoon lemon juice

1 Heat 1 tablespoon of the oil in large saucepan; cook chicken, in batches, until browned. Remove from pan.
2 Heat remaining oil in same pan; cook onion, garlic and mushrooms, stirring, about 5 minutes or until mushrooms soften. Add stock, the water, cauliflower and potato; bring to the boil. Reduce heat; simmer, uncovered, 20 minutes. Remove from heat; stand 10 minutes.
3 Using hand-held blender, process soup in pan until smooth. Return chicken to pan with cream; stir over medium heat until hot.
4 Serve bowls of soup drizzled with combined pesto and juice.

PASTA, BACON AND VEGETABLE SOUP

prep + cook time **1 hour 25 minutes** serves **6**
nutritional count per serving **18.5g total fat (5.3g saturated fat); 1760kJ (421 cal); 32.6g carbohydrate; 27.5g protein; 6.8g fibre**

2 tablespoons olive oil
1 small brown onion (80g), chopped finely
6 rindless bacon slices (390g), chopped coarsely
2.5 litres (10 cups) water
1kg bacon bones
2 tablespoons tomato paste
3 medium potatoes (600g), quartered
300g piece pumpkin, chopped coarsely
200g cauliflower, chopped coarsely
2½ cups (200g) finely shredded cabbage
1 medium carrot (120g), chopped coarsely
1 cup (110g) frozen beans
1 large zucchini (150g), chopped coarsely
¾ cup (95g) small pasta shells

1 Heat oil in large saucepan; cook onion and bacon slices, stirring, until onion softens.
2 Add the water, bacon bones, paste, potato, pumpkin and cauliflower; bring to the boil. Reduce heat; simmer, covered, 45 minutes.
3 Remove and discard bacon bones. Using potato masher, roughly crush vegetables.
4 Add cabbage, carrot, beans, zucchini and pasta; simmer, uncovered, about 10 minutes or until pasta is cooked.

pasta, bacon and vegetable soup

CREAM OF CHICKEN SOUP

prep + cook time **3 hours 15 minutes** serves **4**
nutritional count per serving (incl. damper)
67.6g total fat (19.2g saturated fat); 4460kJ (1067 cal); 51.6g carbohydrate; 61.1g protein; 4.6g fibre

2 litres (8 cups) water
1 litre (4 cups) chicken stock
1.8kg whole chicken
1 medium carrot (120g), chopped coarsely
1 stalk celery (150g), trimmed, chopped coarsely
1 medium brown onion (150g), chopped coarsely
40g butter
⅓ cup (50g) plain flour
2 tablespoons lemon juice
½ cup (125ml) cream
¼ cup finely chopped fresh flat-leaf parsley

1 Place the water and stock in large saucepan with chicken, carrot, celery and onion; bring to the boil. Reduce heat; simmer, covered, 1½ hours. Remove chicken from pan; simmer broth, covered, 30 minutes.
2 Strain broth through muslin-lined sieve or colander into large heatproof bowl; discard solids. Remove and discard chicken skin and bones; shred meat coarsely.
3 Make herb and cheese damper.
4 Melt butter in large saucepan, add flour; cook, stirring, until mixture thickens and bubbles. Gradually stir in broth and juice; bring to the boil, stirring. Add cream, reduce heat; simmer, uncovered, about 25 minutes, stirring occasionally. Add chicken; stir soup over medium heat until hot.
5 Serve bowls of soup sprinkled with parsley, accompanied with damper.

herb and cheese damper
Preheat oven to 200°C/180°C fan-forced. Heat 2 teaspoons olive oil in saucepan; cook 1 finely chopped small brown onion until soft. Cool. Sift 1⅓ cups self-raising flour into medium bowl; add onion, ⅓ cup grated cheddar cheese and 2 tablespoons each finely chopped fresh flat-leaf parsley and chives. Stir in as much of ⅔ cup milk required to mix to a soft, sticky dough; turn onto floured surface, knead until smooth. Shape into four equal rounds. Place on oiled oven tray; sprinkle with 2 tablespoons grated parmesan cheese. Bake 20 minutes or until browned lightly.

seafood chowder

SEAFOOD CHOWDER

prep + cook time **50 minutes** serves **4**
nutritional count per serving **23.7g total fat (13.1g saturated fat); 2061kJ (493 cal); 15.8g carbohydrate; 53.3g protein; 1.4g fibre**

300g small mussels
500g uncooked medium prawns
40g butter
1 small leek (200g), sliced thinly
2 cloves garlic, crushed
2 rindless bacon slices (130g), chopped finely
2 tablespoons plain flour
3 cups (750ml) milk
1 cup (250ml) vegetable stock
200g baby squid hoods, sliced thinly
300g firm white fish fillets, chopped coarsely
2 tablespoons finely chopped fresh chives

1 Scrub mussels; remove beards. Shell and devein prawns, leaving tails intact.
2 Melt butter in large saucepan; cook leek, garlic and bacon, stirring, until leek softens.
3 Add flour to pan; cook, stirring 1 minute. Stir in milk and stock; bring to the boil. Reduce heat; simmer, uncovered, 10 minutes.
4 Add seafood; simmer, uncovered, about 4 minutes or until prawns change colour and mussels open (discard any that do not). Serve chowder sprinkled with chives.

FRENCH ONION SOUP WITH GRUYERE CROUTONS

prep + cook time **1 hour 10 minutes** serves **4**
nutritional count per serving **16.7g total fat (10g saturated fat); 1522kJ (364 cal); 31.1g carbohydrate; 13.4g protein; 3.9g fibre**

50g butter
4 large brown onions (800g), sliced thinly
¾ cup (180ml) dry white wine
3 cups (750ml) water
1 litre (4 cups) beef stock
1 dried bay leaf
1 tablespoon plain flour
1 teaspoon fresh thyme leaves
gruyère croûtons
1 small french bread (150g), cut in 1.5cm slices
½ cup (60g) coarsely grated gruyère cheese

1 Melt butter in large saucepan; cook onion, stirring occasionally, about 30 minutes or until caramelised.
2 Meanwhile, bring wine to the boil in large saucepan; boil 1 minute then stir in the water, stock and bay leaf; return to the boil. Remove from heat.
3 Stir flour into onion mixture; cook, stirring, 2 minutes. Gradually add hot broth mixture to onion mixture, stirring, until mixture boils and thickens slightly. Reduce heat; simmer, uncovered, stirring occasionally, 20 minutes. Discard bay leaf; stir in thyme.
4 Meanwhile, make gruyère croûtons.
5 Serve bowls of soup topped with croûtons. Sprinkle with extra thyme leaves, if you like.
gruyère croûtons Preheat grill. Toast bread on one side then turn and sprinkle with cheese; grill croûtons until cheese browns lightly.

french onion soup with gruyère croûtons

BOUILLABAISSE WITH ROUILLE

prep + cook time **1 hour 40 minutes** serves **6**
nutritional count per serving **17.3g total fat (2.9g saturated fat); 2132kJ (510 cal); 29.5g carbohydrate; 48.9g protein; 6.2g fibre**

700g uncooked large prawns
2 uncooked medium blue swimmer crabs (650g)
10 small tomatoes (900g)
1 tablespoon olive oil
1 clove garlic, crushed
1 large brown onion (200g), chopped coarsely
1 medium leek (350g), chopped coarsely
1 baby fennel bulb (130g), chopped coarsely
1 fresh small red thai chilli, chopped coarsely
1 dried bay leaf
pinch saffron threads
10cm strip fresh orange peel
1.5 litres (6 cups) water
1 cup (250ml) dry white wine
750g firm white fish fillets, chopped coarsely
500g small black mussels
½ cup coarsely chopped fresh flat-leaf parsley
1 small french bread (150g)

rouille
1 medium red capsicum (200g)
1 fresh small red thai chilli, chopped coarsely
1 clove garlic, quartered
1 cup (70g) stale breadcrumbs
1 tablespoon lemon juice
¼ cup (60ml) olive oil

1 Shell and devein prawns, leaving tails intact. Reserve heads and shells; place prawn meat in medium bowl.
2 Slide a knife under top of crab shell at back, lever off shell; reserve with prawn shells. Discard gills; rinse crabs under cold water. Cut crab bodies into quarters; add to bowl of prawn meat.
3 Chop four of the tomatoes coarsely; reserve with seafood shells. Peel remaining tomatoes; remove seeds. Chop flesh finely.
4 Heat oil in large saucepan; cook reserved seafood shell mixture, garlic, onion, leek, fennel, chilli, bay leaf, saffron and peel, stirring, about 10 minutes or until shells change colour and vegetables soften. Add the water and wine, cover; bring to the boil. Reduce heat; simmer, covered, 10 minutes. Remove and discard crab shells.
5 Blend or process seafood mixture (including prawn shells), in batches, until smooth; using a wooden spoon, push each batch through a large sieve into large saucepan. Discard solids in sieve. Reserve ¼ cup strained seafood mixture for rouille.
6 Make rouille.
7 Add finely chopped tomatoes to strained liquid; bring to the boil. Add fish and mussels, return to the boil; cook, covered, 5 minutes. Add reserved prawn meat and crab pieces; cook, covered, 5 minutes. Stir parsley into soup.
8 Preheat grill. Cut bread into slices; toast under grill until browned lightly.
9 Serve soup with toast and rouille.

rouille Quarter capsicum; discard seeds and membrane. Roast under preheated grill or in very hot oven, skin-side up, until skin blisters and blackens. Cover capsicum pieces with plastic or paper for 5 minutes then peel away skin; chop coarsely. Blend or process capsicum with chilli, garlic, breadcrumbs, juice and reserved strained seafood mixture liquid until smooth. With motor operating, gradually add oil in a thin, steady stream; process until rouille thickens.

clam chowder

CLAM CHOWDER

prep + cook time **35 minutes (+ standing)** serves **4**
nutritional count per serving **19.4g total fat (8.8g saturated fat); 1672kJ (400 cal); 28.7g carbohydrate; 26.4g protein; 2.5g fibre**

1kg baby clams
2 tablespoons coarse cooking salt
40g butter
1 large brown onion (200g), chopped coarsely
2 rindless bacon slices (130g), chopped coarsely
1 clove garlic, crushed
2 tablespoons plain flour
3 cups (750ml) milk, warmed
2 cups (500ml) vegetable stock, warmed
2 medium potatoes (400g), chopped coarsely
2 tablespoons chopped fresh chives

1 Rinse clams under cold water. Place in large bowl; sprinkle with salt, cover with water. Stand 1 hour; rinse, drain.
2 Meanwhile, melt butter in large saucepan; cook onion, bacon and garlic, stirring, until onion softens. Add flour to pan; cook, stirring, until mixture thickens and bubbles. Gradually stir in milk and stock; stir until mixture boils and thickens slightly. Add potato, reduce heat; simmer, covered, until potato is tender.
3 Add clams; simmer, covered, 5 minutes or until clams open (discard any that do not). Sprinkle chowder with chives; serve with grilled slices of bread.

MEDITERRANEAN FISH SOUP

prep + cook time **55 minutes** serves **4**
nutritional count per serving **7.7g total fat (1.4g saturated fat); 978kJ (234 cal); 8.5g carbohydrate; 28.3g protein; 3.7g fibre**

1 tablespoon olive oil
1 clove garlic, crushed
1 small leek (200g), halved, sliced thinly
1 small red capsicum (150g), cut into 1cm pieces
1 small red onion (100g), halved, sliced thinly
1 stalk celery (150g), trimmed, cut into 1cm pieces
1 small carrot (70g), cut into 1cm pieces
½ teaspoon finely grated orange rind
¼ teaspoon dried chilli flakes
2 tablespoons tomato paste
2 cups (500ml) water
3 cups (750ml) fish stock
¼ cup (60ml) dry white wine
2 large egg tomatoes (180g), chopped
200g uncooked small king prawns
200g skinless blue-eye fillet, chopped coarsely
200g skinless ocean trout fillet, chopped coarsely
¼ teaspoon finely chopped fresh thyme
1 tablespoon finely chopped fresh dill

1 Heat oil in large saucepan; cook garlic, leek, capsicum, onion, celery, carrot, rind and chilli, stirring, until vegetables soften.
2 Add paste, the water, stock, wine and tomato; bring to the boil. Reduce heat; simmer, uncovered, 20 minutes.
3 Meanwhile, shell and devein prawns; chop meat coarsely. Add prawn meat, fish, thyme and half the dill to soup; simmer, uncovered, 3 minutes or until prawn and fish are cooked.
4 Serve bowls of soup sprinkled with remaining dill.

mediterranean fish soup

ASIAN BEEF CONSOMME

prep + cook time **40 minutes** serves **4**

Heat 1 tablespoon of peanut oil in large saucepan until very hot; stir-fry 300g beef strips with 1 chopped red thai chilli and a teaspoon or two of grated fresh ginger until the beef is browned. Pour in a litre of beef consommé or stock; bring to the boil then simmer about 30 minutes with the lid on. While the beef is cooking, soak 125g bean thread vermicelli for about 5 minutes in a bowl of boiling water, drain then divide among serving bowls. Add a small bunch of roughly chopped baby buk choy and 2 tablespoons of lime juice to the soup; heat until buk choy wilts then pour soup over the vermicelli.

BEEF AND VEGETABLE SOUP WITH POTATO DUMPLINGS

prep + cook time **40 minutes** serves **4**

Boil or microwave a large chopped potato until tender then mash it with an egg yolk, a few teaspoons of chopped chives and 2 tablespoons each of flour and grated cheddar cheese. Shape tablespoons of potato mixture into patties and coat them in packaged breadcrumbs. Heat about ¼ cup of vegetable oil in frying pan; cook dumplings until browned lightly both sides then drain well on absorbent paper. Heat two 505g cans of beef and vegetable soup and a cup of water in large saucepan until hot (do not boil). Serve bowls of soup topped with potato dumplings.

ASIAN-INSPIRED

THAI CHICKEN, PUMPKIN AND COCONUT SOUP

prep + cook time **20 minutes** serves **4**

Buy a large barbecued chicken weighing about 900g; discard the skin and carcass then chop the meat roughly. Stir ¼ cup red curry paste in a large heated saucepan until it's fragrant. Add two 420g cans cream of pumpkin soup, 3¼ cups light coconut milk and 1½ cups chicken stock to the pan and bring to the boil. Stir in the chicken; reduce heat to medium then stir until soup is heated through. Stir in 4 thinly sliced green onions and about a ¼ cup of roughly chopped basil leaves just before serving.

CHINESE CHICKEN AND CORN SOUP

prep + cook time **20 minutes** serves **4**

Buy a large barbecued chicken weighing about 900g; discard the skin and carcass then chop the meat roughly. Heat 1 teaspoon of vegetable oil in a large saucepan; cook 1 teaspoon freshly grated ginger and 2 thinly sliced green chillies about 2 minutes. Add two 505g cans chicken and sweet corn soup and 2½ cups water. Stir in chicken; bring to the boil, then simmer. Beat 1 egg white in a small jug with 1 tablespoon of cold water; slowly pour into the soup, stirring constantly. Serve soup sprinkled with sliced green onion.

MOROCCAN VEGETABLE AND HARISSA SOUP

prep + cook time **25 minutes** serves **4**

Heat 2 teaspoons of olive oil in a large saucepan; stir in 2 crushed garlic cloves until fragrant. Add ¼ cup couscous, 2 tablespoons harissa and 250g fresh halved cherry tomatoes and stir over medium heat for a minute or two. Add two 420g cans vegetable soup and 2½ cups water; bring to the boil then reduce heat and simmer soup, uncovered, about 5 minutes or until the couscous is just softened. Serve bowls of soup sprinkled with ¼ cup roasted pine nuts and a little finely chopped fresh coriander.

PUMPKIN SOUP WITH CHILLI-CRUSTED PEPITAS

prep + cook time **35 minutes** serves **4**

Preheat oven to 180°C/160°C fan-forced. Combine ½ cup pepitas,1 teaspoon dried chilli flakes, 1 teaspoon finely grated lemon rind and 2 teaspoons olive oil in small bowl. Place pepita mixture on an oven tray; roast, uncovered, about 25 minutes or until pepitas are browned lightly. Heat two 505g cans butternut pumpkin soup in a medium saucepan, stirring; serve bowls of soup sprinkled with pepitas.

MEDITERRANEAN-INSPIRED

POTATO, BACON AND LEEK SOUP WITH BLUE CHEESE TOASTS

prep + cook time **30 minutes** serves **4**

Preheat grill. Slice a small french bread stick into 10 even pieces (discard both ends). Toast on one side then turn and top untoasted side with combined 100g crumbled blue cheese and 2 thinly sliced green onions; grill until cheese melts. Chop two rindlesss bacon slices, browning them in a medium saucepan before adding 2 finely chopped green onions and 2 cloves crushed garlic; cook, stirring, until just soft. Add two 505g cans potato and leek soup, ½ cup milk and ¼ cup water; stir until hot. Serve soup with toasts.

ITALIAN TOMATO, BEAN AND BASIL SOUP

prep + cook time **20 minutes** serves **4**

Heat 2 teaspoons of olive oil in a small frying pan and cook a chopped medium onion, 2 crushed garlic cloves and ⅓ cup fresh basil leaves, stirring, until onion is soft. Blend this mixture with 420g can condensed tomato soup, 1¾ cups water and 85g chopped roasted red capsicum until smooth. Combine soup mixture in a saucepan with 425g can rinsed and drained white beans. Bring mixture to the boil; simmer, uncovered, about 5 minutes. Stir in ⅓ cup cream and serve bowls of soup sprinkled with fresh baby basil leaves.

AVOCADO, OLIVE AND BOCCONCINI BRUSCHETTA

prep + cook time 20 minutes **serves** 4
nutritional count per serving 28.8g total fat (6.8g saturated fat); 1693kJ (405 cal); 24.4g carbohydrate; 10.1g protein; 4.5g fibre

¼ cup (60ml) olive oil
2 cloves garlic, crushed
4 slices (180g) wholegrain bread
1 medium avocado (250g), chopped coarsely
100g bocconcini cheese, chopped coarsely
¼ cup (30g) seeded black olives, chopped coarsely
1 tablespoon lemon juice
2 medium tomatoes (300g), chopped coarsely

1 Preheat grill.
2 Combine half the oil and half the garlic in small bowl. Brush both sides of bread with garlic oil; toast under hot grill until browned lightly both sides.
3 Combine avocado, cheese, olives, juice, tomato and remaining oil and garlic in medium bowl.
4 Top bruschetta with avocado mixture.

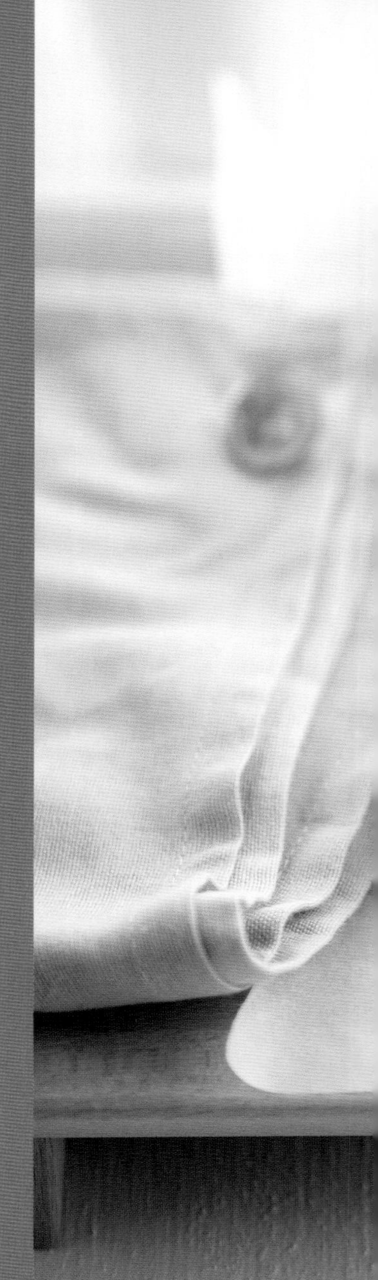

ACCOMPANIMENTS

cheesy pastry twists

CHEESY PASTRY TWISTS

prep + cook time **30 minutes** makes **24**
nutritional count per twist **4.8g total fat (1.2g saturated fat); 314kJ (75 cal); 5g carbohydrate; 2.7g protein; 0.2g fibre**

2 sheets puff pastry, thawed
1 egg yolk, beaten lightly
1 cup (100g) coarsely grated pizza cheese
½ cup (40g) finely grated parmesan cheese

1 Preheat oven to 200°C/180°C fan-forced. Oil two oven trays; line with baking paper.
2 Brush one pastry sheet with half the egg yolk; sprinkle with pizza cheese. Top with remaining pastry sheet; brush with remaining egg yolk. Sprinkle with parmesan cheese.
3 Cut pastry stack in half; place one pastry half on top of the other, pressing down firmly.
4 Cut pastry widthways into 24 strips; twist each, pinching ends to seal. Place twists on trays.
5 Bake, uncovered, about 10 minutes or until browned lightly.

OLIVE LOAF

prep + cook time **50 minutes** serves **6**
nutritional count per serving **21.3g total fat (11.2g saturated fat); 1371kJ (328 cal); 22.5g carbohydrate; 12.1g protein; 1.5g fibre**

1 cup (150g) self-raising flour
⅔ cup (50g) coarsely grated parmesan cheese
2 tablespoons coarsely chopped fresh mint
½ teaspoon ground black pepper
1 cup (120g) seeded black olives, chopped coarsely
75g mortadella, chopped coarsely
4 eggs, beaten lightly
80g butter, melted

1 Preheat oven to 200°C/180°C fan-forced. Oil 8cm x 26cm bar cake pan.
2 Sift flour into medium bowl; stir in cheese, mint, pepper, olives and mortadella. Add egg and butter; stir until well combined.
3 Spread mixture into pan; bake about 35 minutes or until browned lightly. Serve loaf warm.

tips **Can be made a day ahead; keep, covered, in the refrigerator. Loaf is also suitable to freeze; thaw overnight in the refrigerator then reheat in the oven before serving.**

olive loaf

cheese, corn and bacon muffins

CHEESE, CORN AND BACON MUFFINS

prep + cook time **40 minutes (+ standing)** makes **12**
nutritional count per muffin **12.2g total fat (7g saturated fat); 1045kJ (250 cal); 25.7g carbohydrate; 8.2g protein; 1.9g fibre**

½ cup (85g) polenta
½ cup (125ml) milk
3 rindless bacon slices (210g), chopped finely
4 green onions, chopped finely
1½ cups (225g) self-raising flour
1 tablespoon caster sugar
310g can corn kernels, rinsed, drained
125g can creamed corn
100g butter, melted
2 eggs, beaten lightly
50g piece cheddar cheese
¼ cup (30g) coarsely grated cheddar cheese

1 Preheat oven to 200°C/180°C fan-forced. Grease 12-hole (½-cup/80ml) muffin pan.
2 Mix polenta and milk in small bowl, cover; stand 20 minutes.
3 Cook bacon in heated oiled small frying pan 2 minutes. Add onion; cook, stirring, 2 minutes. Remove pan from heat; cool bacon mixture.
4 Sift flour and sugar into large bowl; stir in corn kernels, creamed corn and bacon mixture. Add melted butter, egg and polenta mixture; mix muffin batter only until just combined.
5 Spoon 1 tablespoon of the batter into each pan hole. Cut piece of cheese into 12 equal pieces; place one piece in the centre of each pan hole. Divide remaining batter among pan holes; sprinkle grated cheese over each.
6 Bake, uncovered, in oven about 20 minutes or until muffins are well risen. Turn muffins onto wire rack. Serve muffins warm.

mini muffin dampers

MINI MUFFIN DAMPERS

prep + cook time **35 minutes** makes **12**
nutritional count per damper **7.8g total fat (4.3g saturated fat); 924kJ (221 cal); 29.2g carbohydrate; 7.6g protein; 1.5g fibre**

3 cups (450g) self-raising flour
40g butter, chopped
1¾ cups (430ml) buttermilk
2 tablespoons basil pesto
¾ cup (90g) coarsely grated cheddar cheese
¼ teaspoon sweet paprika
1 tablespoon plain flour

1 Preheat oven to 200°C/180°C fan-forced. Grease 12-hole (⅓-cup/80ml) muffin pan.
2 Place self-raising flour in large bowl; rub in butter with fingertips. Using fork, stir in buttermilk to form a soft, sticky dough. Swirl pesto and cheese through; do not overmix.
3 Divide mixture among pan holes. Sprinkle with combined paprika and plain flour. Bake 25 minutes. Turn muffins onto wire rack; serve muffins warm.
tip **Sun-dried tomato pesto can also be used.**

farmhouse spinach and double cheese plait

FARMHOUSE SPINACH AND DOUBLE CHEESE PLAIT

prep + cook time **1 hour 15 minutes (+ cooling)**
serves **10**
nutritional count per serving **8.8g total fat (5.5g saturated fat); 924kJ (221 cal); 23.4g carbohydrate; 16g protein; 2.5g fibre**

600g spinach, trimmed
15g butter
1 medium leek (350g), chopped finely
2 teaspoons chopped fresh thyme
2 cups (300g) self-raising flour
1 cup (80g) finely grated parmesan cheese
¼ cup finely chopped fresh basil
¾ cup (150g) fetta cheese, crumbled
1 cup (250ml) milk, approximately

1 Preheat oven to 200°C/180°C fan-forced.
2 Add spinach to large saucepan of boiling water; boil 1 minute, drain. Rinse under cold water; drain well. Squeeze excess moisture from spinach, chop finely.
3 Heat butter in pan, add leek and thyme; cook, stirring occasionally, until leek is soft. Add spinach; cook, stirring, about 5 minutes or until any liquid has evaporated, cool.
4 Sift flour into medium bowl; stir in parmesan, basil, three-quarters of the fetta, spinach mixture and enough milk to mix to a soft, sticky dough.
5 Turn dough onto floured surface, knead until smooth. Divide dough into 3 pieces, shape into 36cm sausages. Plait sausages together; place on greased oven tray, sprinkle with remaining fetta. Bake, in oven, about 40 minutes; serve warm.

RICOTTA, BASIL AND PINE NUT PIZZA

prep + cook time **25 minutes** serves **4**
nutritional count per serving **16.3g total fat (5.1g saturated fat); 1760kJ (421 cal); 50.2g carbohydrate; 16.7g protein; 4.8g fibre**

4 large pitta breads (320g)
1 cup (260g) bottled tomato pasta sauce
1 cup (240g) ricotta cheese
¼ cup (40g) roasted pine nuts
1 cup loosely packed fresh basil leaves
50g baby spinach leaves

1 Preheat oven to 220°C/200°C fan-forced.
2 Place bread on oven trays; spread with sauce. Divide cheese and nuts among bread.
3 Cook, uncovered, about 10 minutes or until bases are crisp and topping is heated through; serve topped with basil and spinach leaves.

ricotta, basil and pine nut pizza

PUMPKIN AND CORN ROLL

prep + cook time **1 hour 15 minutes (+ cooling)**
serves **10**
nutritional count per serving **8.6g total fat (5.2g saturated fat); 744kJ (178 cal); 20.5g carbohydrate; 3.4g protein; 2.3g fibre**

90g butter, softened
⅓ cup (75g) firmly packed brown sugar
1 egg
125g can corn kernels, rinsed, drained
½ cup (125g) cold mashed pumpkin
1 cup (160g) wholemeal self-raising flour
2 tablespoons milk

1 Adjust oven shelves to fit upright nut roll tins. Preheat oven to 170°C/150°C fan-focred. Grease lids and inside of 8cm x 20cm nut roll tin evenly with melted butter; place base lid on tin, position tin upright on oven tray.
2 Beat butter and sugar in small bowl with electric mixer until light and fluffy. Beat in egg then stir in remaining ingredients. Spoon mixture into tin; tap tin firmly on bench to remove any air pockets; position top lid.
3 Bake roll about 1 hour. Stand loaf in tin 5 minutes; remove lids, shake tin gently to release loaf onto wire rack to cool.

tips **You need to cook about 400g pumpkin to make enough mashed pumpkin for this recipe.**
The tin needs to be coated thickly with melted butter so the roll won't stick to the inside of the tin. Don't use cooking-oil spray, as this doesn't give a good enough coating and the roll will stick and be hard to turn out.
note **If you can't find nut roll tins, this mixture can be baked – at the same temperature as above – in a greased and lined 15cm x 25cm loaf pan for about 1¼ hours. Spoon the mixture into the loaf pan, cover pan with a strip of pleated foil (the pleat allows the loaf to rise evenly), and bake for 1 hour, then remove the foil and bake about a further 15 minutes.**

garlic bread

GARLIC BREAD

prep + cook time **10 minutes** serves **4**
nutritional count per serving **11.2g total fat (5.9g saturated fat); 1229kJ (294 cal); 38.9g carbohydrate; 7.9g protein; 2.6g fibre**

1 loaf turkish bread (430g)
50g butter, melted
2 cloves garlic, crushed
2 tablespoons finely chopped fresh flat-leaf parsley

1 Halve bread horizontally; cut each half into four pieces.
2 Combine butter, garlic and parsley in small bowl; brush over bread pieces.
3 Cook bread on heated oiled grill plate (or grill or barbecue), uncovered, until browned both sides.

CHEESY BUTTERMILK SCONES

prep + cook time **35 minutes** makes **8**
nutritional count per serving **8.6g total fat (5.5g saturated fat); 765kJ (183 cal); 19.8g carbohydrate; 6.1g protein; 1g fibre**

1½ cups (225g) self-raising flour
50g butter, chopped coarsely
⅓ cup (40g) coarsely grated cheddar cheese
⅓ cup (25g) coarsely grated parmesan cheese
¼ teaspoon cayenne pepper
¾ cup (180ml) buttermilk

1 Preheat oven to 220°C/200°C fan-forced. Grease shallow 20cm-round cake pan.
2 Sift flour into large bowl; rub in butter. Stir in cheddar cheese, half of the parmesan cheese and the cayenne pepper.
3 Add buttermilk to flour mixture; use a knife to cut buttermilk through the mixture to make a soft, sticky dough. Turn dough onto floured surface; knead lightly until smooth.
4 Press dough into an even 2cm thickness. Dip 5.5cm-round cutter into flour; cut as many rounds as possible from dough. Place scones side by side, just touching, in pan.
5 Gently knead scraps of dough together; repeat pressing and cutting of dough, place in pan. Sprinkle tops with remaining parmesan cheese. Bake about 20 minutes.

cheesy buttermilk scones

kumara dampers

KUMARA DAMPERS

prep + cook time **50 minutes** makes **4**
nutritional count per damper **5.2g total fat (3.2g saturated fat); 543kJ (130 cal); 56.5g carbohydrate; 2.8g protein; 1.5g fibre**

1⅔ cups (225g) gluten-free self-raising flour
1 teaspoon caster sugar
¼ teaspoon salt
20g butter
½ cup cold mashed sieved cooked kumara
½ cup (125ml) buttermilk
2 tablespoons water, approximately
2 teaspoons milk, approximately
2 teaspoons gluten-free self-raising flour, extra

1 Preheat oven to 220°C/200°C fan-forced. Grease oven tray.
2 Sift dry ingredients into large bowl; rub in the butter. Add kumara, buttermilk and enough of the water to mix to a soft, sticky dough. Knead dough lightly on floured surface until smooth.
3 Divide dough into four equal portions. Roll each portion into rounds, place on tray. Cut cross through top of dough, about 5mm deep. Brush tops with milk, then dust with extra sifted flour.
4 Bake dampers about 35 minutes.

tip **You will need to cook 250g kumara for this recipe.**
storage **Dampers are best made and eaten on the same day. They can be frozen for up to 3 months. Thaw in the oven, wrapped in foil.**

sun-dried tomato and bacon scrolls

SUN-DRIED TOMATO AND BACON SCROLLS

prep + cook time **40 minutes** makes **12**
nutritional count per scroll **5.2g total fat (3.2g saturated fat); 1229kJ (294 cal); 57.3g carbohydrate; 2.6g protein; 1.3g fibre**

2 cups (300g) self-raising flour
1 tablespoon caster sugar
50g cold butter, chopped coarsely
¾ cup (180ml) milk
¼ cup (65g) sun-dried tomato pesto
1 cup (120g) pizza cheese
3 rindless bacon slices (210g), chopped finely
2 tablespoons finely chopped fresh chives

1 Preheat oven to 200°C/180°C fan-forced. Grease shallow 22cm-square cake pan.
2 Sift flour and sugar into medium bowl; rub in butter. Add milk; mix to a soft, sticky dough. Turn dough onto floured surface; knead until smooth. Roll dough in a 30cm x 40cm rectangle.
3 Spread dough with pesto; sprinkle with combined cheese, bacon and chives. Roll dough tightly from long side. Using serrated knife, trim ends. Cut roll into 12 slices; place, cut-side up, in pan. Bake about 25 minutes.

brie and quince matchsticks

BRIE AND QUINCE MATCHSTICKS

prep + cook time **20 minutes** makes **10**
nutritional count per matchstick **11.1g total fat (6.7g saturated fat); 648kJ (155 cal); 8g carbohydrate; 5.8g protein; 0.4g fibre**

1 sheet puff pastry
250g wedge brie cheese
10 small sprigs fresh lemon thyme
2 tablespoons quince paste

1 Preheat oven to 220°C/200°C fan-forced.
2 Cut pastry into ten 12cm x 4.5cm rectangles. Cut cheese into 10 slices. Place pastry rectangles on greased oven tray; pierce with fork. Bake about 10 minutes.
3 Top hot matchsticks with cheese, thyme and quince paste. Serve warm.

CARROT AND ZUCCHINI MUFFINS

prep + cook time **30 minutes** makes **12**
nutritional count per muffin **9.4g total fat (5.6g saturated fat); 932kJ (223 cal); 28.1g carbohydrate; 5.7g protein; 1.4g fibre**

2 cups (300g) self-raising flour
½ cup (110g) firmly packed brown sugar
1 teaspoon ground cumin
½ teaspoon bicarbonate of soda
1 cup (110g) lightly packed, coarsely grated carrot
1 cup (110g) lightly packed, coarsely grated zucchini
½ cup (60g) coarsely grated cheddar cheese
2 eggs
¾ cup (180ml) buttermilk
90g butter, melted

1 Preheat oven to 200°C/180°C fan-forced. Line 12-hole (⅓-cup/80ml) muffin pan with paper cases.
2 Sift flour, sugar, cumin and soda into large bowl; stir in carrot, zucchini and cheese then eggs, buttermilk and butter. Do not over-mix; mixture should be lumpy.
3 Drop ¼ cups of mixture into paper cases; bake about 20 minutes. Stand muffins in pan 5 minutes before turning, top-side up, onto wire rack to cool.
tip **You need 2 medium carrots (240g) and 2 small zucchini (180g) for this recipe.**

carrot and zucchini muffins

ZUCCHINI, OLIVE AND TOMATO POLENTA FINGERS

prep + cook time **25 minutes (+ refrigeration)** makes **12**
nutritional count per finger **4.5g total fat (1g saturated fat); 439kJ (105 cal); 12.7g carbohydrate; 2.9g protein; 1.1g fibre**

2 cups (500ml) water
2 cups (500ml) chicken stock
1 cup (170g) polenta
1 large zucchini (150g), grated coarsely
½ cup (80g) coarsely chopped seeded black olives
⅓ cup (25g) finely grated parmesan cheese
¼ cup (35g) semi-dried tomatoes in oil, drained, chopped finely
2 tablespoons olive oil

1 Grease deep 19cm-square cake pan; line base and sides with baking paper.
2 Bring the water and stock to the boil in large saucepan; gradually stir in polenta. Reduce heat; simmer, stirring, about 10 minutes or until polenta thickens. Stir in zucchini, olives, cheese and tomato. Spread polenta mixture into pan; cover, refrigerate about 1 hour or until polenta is firm.
3 Turn polenta onto board; cut in half. Cut each half into six slices.
4 Heat oil in large frying pan; cook polenta, until browned both sides.

tip **Cooked polenta fingers can be stored in an airtight container in the refrigerator for up to 3 days. Polenta fingers can be eaten cold or reheated in the microwave on HIGH (100%) for 30 seconds.**

CHEESY CORIANDER PESTO KNOTS

prep + cook time **40 minutes** makes **10**
nutritional count per knot **16g total fat (5g saturated fat); 1191kJ (285 cal); 26.3g carbohydrate; 8.1g protein; 1.8g fibre**

2¼ cups (335g) self-raising flour
2 teaspoons caster sugar
¼ teaspoon salt
30g butter, chopped
1 cup (250ml) milk, approximately
100g hard goat's cheese
ground black pepper
pesto
⅔ cup firmly packed fresh coriander leaves
½ cup (40g) coarsely grated parmesan cheese
½ cup (80g) roasted pine nuts
1 clove garlic, crushed
2 tablespoons olive oil
1 tablespoon water

1 Preheat oven to 240°C/220°C fan-forced.
2 Make pesto.
3 Sift flour, sugar and salt into medium bowl; rub in butter with fingertips. Stir in enough milk to mix to a soft, sticky dough.
4 Turn dough onto floured surface; knead until smooth. Roll dough to 17cm x 30cm rectangle. Spread dough with pesto; top with crumbled cheese, sprinkle with pepper.
5 Cut dough crossways into 3cm strips. Hold both ends of dough strip in each hand, loop dough as if to make a knot; tuck ends under neatly. Place knots on greased oven trays about 2cm apart. Bake about 15 minutes; serve warm.
pesto Process coriander, cheese, nuts and garlic until combined. With motor operating, gradually add oil in a thin, steady stream; add water, process until smooth.

ANCHOVY TOASTS

prep + cook time **15 minutes** makes **8**

Combine 6 finely chopped anchovy fillets, 2 tablespoons finely chopped fresh garlic chives and 60g softened butter in a bowl. Preheat grill. Toast 8 slices french bread stick on one side under grill. Spread untoasted side with anchovy butter; grill until browned lightly.

GRUYERE TOASTS

prep + cook time **10 minutes** makes **8**

Preheat grill. Cut half a french bread stick into 8 thick slices; toast slices on one side under grill. Turn slices and sprinkle with ⅔ cup finely grated gruyère cheese; grill until cheese melts.

TOASTS

BACON TOASTS

prep + cook time **20 minutes** makes **8**

Preheat grill. Thinly slice half a loaf of ciabatta; toast slices on one side under grill. Turn slices and spread with 2 tablespoons wholegrain mustard. Top with 300g coarsely chopped cooked crisp bacon and sprinkle with ¼ cup finely grated parmesan cheese; grill until browned lightly.

CHILLI PARMESAN CRISPS

prep + cook time **15 minutes** makes **16**

Preheat oven to 220°C/200°C fan-forced. Combine 1 cup finely grated parmesan cheese and ½ finely chopped long red chilli; drop level tablespoons of mixture onto a baking-paper-lined oven tray. Bake about 3 minutes; stand until set.

VEGEMITE CHEESE STRAWS

prep + cook time **30 minutes** makes **24**

Preheat oven to 220°C/200°C fan-forced. Grease oven trays; line with baking paper. Spread 1 sheet puff pastry with 2 teaspoons Vegemite; sprinkle with ⅓ cup finely grated parmesan cheese. Top with another sheet puff pastry; spread with 2 teaspoons Vegemite, then sprinkle with ⅓ cup finely grated parmesan cheese. Cut pastry stack in half; place one stack on top of the other, press down firmly. Cut pastry crossways into 24 strips; twist each strip, pinching ends to seal. Place on trays; bake about 12 minutes or until browned lightly.

SPINACH AND FETTA PINWHEELS

prep + cook time **30 minutes** makes **24**

Preheat oven 220°C/200°C fan-forced. Oil oven trays; line with baking paper. Squeeze excess moisture from 250g thawed frozen spinach. Chop spinach coarsely; pat dry between sheets of absorbent paper. Combine 100g crumbled fetta cheese and ½ cup finely grated parmesan cheese in a small bowl. Sprinkle spinach and combined cheeses over 2 sheets puff pastry. Roll pastry tightly to enclose filling. Cut each roll into 12 slices. Place pinwheels, cut-side up, on trays; brush with a little beaten egg. Bake about 15 minutes or until browned lightly.

PASTRY PIECES

CAPRESE TARTLETS

prep + cook time **30 minutes** makes **9**

Preheat oven to 220°C/200°C fan-forced. Cut nine 7cm rounds from 1 sheet shortcrust pastry. Place rounds on baking-paper-lined oven tray; pierce with fork. Bake about 10 minutes. Spread rounds with 2 tablespoons basil pesto dip. Top rounds with 9 thinly sliced cherry tomatoes and 9 thinly sliced cherry bocconcini cheese. Bake about 2 minutes or until cheese softens. Top each tartlet with a baby basil leaf.

GARLIC PIZZA WEDGES

prep + cook time **25 minutes** makes **32**

Preheat oven to 220°C/200°C fan-forced. Place 2 x 30cm pizza bases on greased oven or pizza trays. Combine 1 tablespoon oil and 2 cloves crushed garlic. Brush pizza bases with oil mixture; sprinkle with 2 tablespoons finely grated parmesan cheese. Bake pizzas about 15 minutes or until browned and crisp. Cut each pizza into 16 wedges.

Soup up your soup with your own stock; the homemade version will add a wonderful flavour – making them even more special. These recipes can be made up to four days ahead and kept, covered, in the refrigerator. They can also be frozen for up to three months.

SPICED YOGURT

prep + cook time **15 minutes** makes **1¼ cups**

Dry-fry 1 teaspoon ground coriander, 1 teaspoon ground cumin and ½ teaspoon hot paprika until fragrant. Combine spices in a small bowl with 1 cup yogurt and ¼ cup finely chopped fresh mint.

DILL CREAM

prep + cook time **10 minutes** makes **½ cup**

Combine ½ cup sour cream with 1 tablespoon finely chopped fresh dill in a small bowl. Dollop on top of soup; sprinkle with extra chopped dill if desired.

BEEF STOCK

prep + cook time **5 hours 10 minutes (+ cooling & refrigeration)** makes **3.5 litres (14 cups)**

Preheat oven to 200°C/180°C fan-forced. Roast 2kg meaty beef bones on oven tray about 1 hour or until browned. Bring 2 chopped medium onions, 5.5 litres water, 2 trimmed chopped celery stalks, 2 chopped medium carrots, 3 bay leaves and 2 teaspoons black peppercorns to the boil in large saucepan or boiler. Simmer, uncovered, 3 hours; skim surface occasionally. Add 3 litres water; simmer, uncovered, 1 hour. Strain stock through muslin-lined sieve into large heatproof bowl; discard solids. Cool, cover; refrigerate until cold. Discard surface fat before using.

VEGETABLE STOCK

prep + cook time **1 hour 40 minutes (+ cooling & refrigeration)** makes **3.5 litres (14 cups)**

Combine 2 chopped large carrots, 2 chopped large parsnips, 4 chopped medium brown onions, 10 trimmed chopped celery stalks, 4 bay leaves, 2 teaspoons black peppercorns and 6 litres water in large saucepan or boiler; simmer, uncovered, 1½ hours. Strain stock through muslin-lined sieve or colander into large heatproof bowl; discard solids. Cool, cover; refrigerate until cold. Discard surface fat before using.

STOCKS & TOPPINGS

GREMOLATA

prep + cook time **10 minutes** makes **⅓ cup**

Combine ⅓ cup finely chopped fresh flat-leaf parsley, 1 tablespoon finely grated lemon rind and 2 cloves finely chopped garlic in a small bowl. Store covered in the fridge.

TORTILLA CRISPS

prep + cook time **15 minutes** makes **1½ cups**

Slice 2 x 15cm corn tortillas into thin strips; shallow-fry in vegetable oil, in batches, until browned lightly. Drain on absorbent paper.

FISH STOCK

prep + cook time **25 minutes (+ cooling & refrigeration)** makes **2.5 litres (10 cups)**

Combine 1.5kg fish bones, 3 litres water, 1 chopped medium onion, 2 trimmed chopped celery stalks, 2 bay leaves and 1 teaspoon black peppercorns in large saucepan or boiler; simmer, uncovered, 20 minutes. Strain stock through muslin-lined sieve or colander into large heatproof bowl; discard solids. Cool, cover; refrigerate until cold. Discard surface fat before using.

CHICKEN STOCK

prep + cook time **2 hours 10 minutes (+ cooling & refrigeration)** makes **3.5 litres (14 cups)**

Combine 2kg chicken bones, 2 chopped medium onions, 2 trimmed chopped celery stalks, 2 medium chopped carrots, 3 bay leaves, 2 teaspoons black peppercorns and 5 litres water in large saucepan or boiler; simmer, uncovered, 2 hours, skimming surface occasionally. Strain stock through muslin-lined sieve or colander into large heatproof bowl; discard solids. Cool, cover; refrigerate until cold. Discard surface fat before using.

BACON SLICES also called bacon rashers.

BAMBOO SHOOTS the tender shoots of bamboo plants, available in cans; rinse and drain before use.

BASIL

sweet the most common type of basil; used extensively in Italian dishes and one of the main ingredients in pesto.

thai has smallish leaves and a sweet licorice/aniseed taste. Available in Asian supermarkets and greengrocers.

BAY LEAVES aromatic leaves from the bay tree available fresh or dried; adds a strong, slightly peppery flavour to dishes.

BEANS

black-eyed also called black-eyed peas or cowpeas. Not too dissimilar to white beans in flavour.

cannellini small, dried white bean similar in appearance and flavour to haricot, navy and great northern beans.

white some recipes may simply call for "white beans", a term we use for canned or dried cannellini, navy, haricot or great northern beans.

BEEF

gravy boneless stewing beef from the shin. Cut crossways, with bone in, is osso buco.

skirt steak lean, flavourful coarse-grained cut from the inner thigh.

BREAD

ciabatta in Italian the word means slipper, the traditional shape of this popular crisp-crusted, open-textured white sourdough bread.

french stick also called baguette. A long, narrow cylindrical loaf with a crisp brown crust and a light chewy centre.

pitta also called lebanese bread; a pocket bread sold in large, flat pieces that separate into two thin rounds.

sourdough so-named, not because it's sour in taste, but because it's made by using a small amount of "starter dough", which contains a yeast culture. Part of the resulting dough is then saved to use as the starter dough next time.

turkish also called pide. Comes in long (about 45cm) flat loaves and individual rounds; made from wheat.

BREADCRUMBS

fresh bread, usually white, processed into crumbs.

packaged prepared fine-textured but crunchy white breadcrumbs; good for coating foods that are to be fried.

BUK CHOY also called bak choy, pak choi, chinese white cabbage or chinese chard; has a fresh, mild mustard taste. Baby buk choy is slightly more tender.

BUTTER we use salted butter unless stated otherwise; 125g is equal to 1 stick (4 ounces).

BUTTERMILK originally the term given to the slightly sour liquid left after butter was churned from cream, today it is made similarly to yogurt. Sold alongside all fresh milk products in supermarkets.

CAPSICUM also known as bell pepper or pepper. Come in many colours: red, green, yellow, orange and purplish-black. Discard seeds and membranes before use.

CAYENNE PEPPER a thin-fleshed, long, extremely hot dried red chilli, usually purchased ground.

CHEESE

bocconcini a walnut-sized, delicate, semi-soft white baby mozzarella cheese. Sold fresh, it spoils rapidly; keep, refrigerated in brine, for one or two days only.

cheddar the most common cow's-milk tasty cheese; should be aged, hard and have a pronounced bite.

fetta a crumbly textured goat's- or sheep-milk cheese having a sharp, salty taste. Is ripened and stored in salted whey.

goat's made from goat's milk, has an earthy, strong taste. Available in soft, crumbly and firm textures, in various shapes and sizes, and may be rolled in ash or herbs.

parmesan also called parmigiano; a hard, grainy cow's-milk cheese that is salted in brine then aged for up to two years.

pizza a commercial blend of grated mozzarella, cheddar and parmesan cheeses.

provolone a stretched-curd cheese similar to mozzarella when young, becoming hard and grainy the longer it's aged. Golden yellow with a smooth waxy rind.

ricotta a soft, sweet, moist, white cows-milk cheese with a low fat content and a slightly grainy texture. Is manufactured from a whey that is itself a by-product of other cheese making.

CHICKPEAS also called garbanzos, hummus or channa; an irregularly round, sandy-coloured legume. Firm texture even after cooking, a floury mouth-feel and robust nutty flavour; available canned or dried (reconstitute for several hours in cold water before use).

CHILLI use rubber gloves when seeding and chopping fresh chillies as they can burn your skin. We use

GLOSSARY

unseeded chillies as the seeds contain the heat; use fewer chillies rather than seeding the lot.

green any unripened chilli; also some varieties that are ripe when green (jalapeño, habanero, serrano).

long red available both fresh and dried; a generic term used for any moderately hot, long, thin chilli (about 6cm to 8cm long).

powder the Asian variety is the hottest, made from dried ground thai chillies; can be used instead of fresh in the proportion of ½ teaspoon chilli powder to 1 medium chopped fresh red chilli.

thai also called "scuds"; tiny, very hot and bright red in colour.

CHIVES related to the onion and leek; has a subtle onion flavour. Used more for flavour than as an ingredient; chopped finely, they're good in sauces, dressings, omelettes or as a garnish.

COCONUT

cream obtained commercially from the first pressing of the coconut flesh alone, without the addition of water. Available in cans and cartons at most supermarkets.

desiccated concentrated, dried, unsweetened and finely shredded coconut flesh.

milk not the liquid found inside the fruit (coconut water), but the diluted liquid from the second pressing of the white flesh of a mature coconut. Available in cans and cartons at most supermarkets.

shredded unsweetened thin strips of dried coconut flesh.

CORIANDER also called cilantro or chinese parsley; bright-green leafy herb with a pungent flavour. The stems and roots are also used.

CUMIN also called zeera or comino; resembling caraway in size, cumin is the dried seed of a plant related to the parsley family. Its spicy, almost curry-like flavour is essential to the traditional foods of Mexico, India, North Africa and the Middle East. Available dried as seeds or ground. Black cumin seeds are smaller than standard cumin, and dark brown rather than true black; they are mistakenly confused with kalonji.

CURRY PASTES are available in various strengths from most supermarkets; adjust the amount you use to suit your taste.

FENNEL also called finocchio or anise. Also the name given to dried seeds having a licorice flavour.

FISH SAUCE also called nam pla or nuoc nam; made from pulverised salted fermented fish (most often anchovies). Has a pungent smell and strong taste. There are many versions of varying intensity, so use according to your taste.

FLOUR

plain also called all-purpose; unbleached wheat flour is the best for baking: the gluten content ensures a strong dough, which produces a light result.

self-raising all-purpose plain or wholemeal flour with baking powder and salt added; make your own by sifting plain flour with baking powder in the proportion of 1 cup flour to 2 teaspoons baking powder.

GINGER

fresh also called root ginger; the thick gnarled root of a tropical plant. Can be kept, peeled, covered with dry sherry in a jar and refrigerated, or frozen in an airtight container.

ground also called powdered ginger; used as a flavouring in baking but cannot be substituted for fresh ginger.

KAFFIR LIME LEAVES also called bai magrood, look like they are two glossy dark green leaves joined end to end forming a rounded hourglass shape. Sold fresh, dried or frozen, the dried leaves are less potent so double the number if using them as a substitute for fresh. A strip of fresh lime peel may be substituted for each kaffir lime leaf.

LEMON GRASS also called takrai, serai or serah. A tall, clumping, lemon-smelling and tasting, sharp-edged aromatic tropical grass; the white lower part of the stem is used, finely chopped.

LENTILS (red, brown, yellow) dried pulses often identified by and named after their colour.

MERGUEZ SAUSAGES small, spicy sausages believed to have originated in Tunisia but eaten throughout North Africa, France and Spain; is traditionally made with lamb meat and is easily recognised because of its chilli-red colour. Can be fried, grilled or roasted; available from many butchers, delicatessens and specialty sausage stores.

MUSHROOMS

button small, cultivated white mushrooms with a mild flavour. When we call for an unspecified type of mushroom, use button.

enoki clumps of long, spaghetti-like stems with tiny, snowy white caps.

oyster also called abalone; grey-white in colour and shaped like a fan. Has a smooth texture and a subtle, oyster-like flavour.

shiitake when fresh, are also called golden oak, forest or chinese black mushrooms; have an earthy taste. When dried are called donko or dried chinese mushrooms; rehydrate before use.
swiss brown also called roman or cremini. Light to dark brown in colour, with a full-bodied flavour.

NOODLES
dried rice also known as rice stick noodles. Made from rice flour and water, available flat and wide or very thin (vermicelli). Must be soaked in boiling water to soften.
fresh rice soft white noodles made from rice flour and vegetable oil; available in varying thicknesses, from thin to broad and flat. Rinse under hot water before using.
soba thin, pale-brown noodle originally from Japan; made from buckwheat and varying proportions of wheat flour. Available dried and fresh, and flavoured.
udon available fresh and dried, these are Japanese broad white wheat noodles.

OIL
cooking spray we use a cholesterol-free cooking spray made from canola oil.
olive made from ripened olives. Extra virgin and virgin are the first and second press, respectively, of the olives and are therefore considered the best; the "extra light" or "light" name on other types refers to taste not fat levels.
sesame made from roasted, crushed, white sesame seeds; used as a flavouring rather than a cooking medium.
vegetable any oils sourced from plant rather than animal fats.

ONION
green also called scallion or, incorrectly, shallot; an immature onion picked before the bulb has formed, having a long, bright-green edible stalk.
red also called spanish or red spanish onion; a sweet-flavoured, large, purple-red onion.
spring crisp, narrow green-leafed tops and a round sweet white bulb larger than green onions.

PARSLEY, FLAT-LEAF also called continental or italian parsley.

PEARL BARLEY a nutritious grain used in soups and stews. Has had the husk removed then is hulled and polished so that only the "pearl" of the original grain remains, much the same as white rice.

POLENTA a flour-like cereal made of ground corn (maize); a fine-textured cornmeal. Also the name of the dish made from it.

RISONI small rice-shape pasta.

SEAFOOD
blue-eye also called deep sea trevalla or trevally and blue-eye cod; thick, moist white-fleshed fish.
clams also called vongole; we use a small ridge-shelled variety of this bivalve mollusc.
ocean trout a farmed fish with pink, soft flesh. It is from the same family as the atlantic salmon; one can be substituted for the other.
prawns also known as shrimp.
white fish means non-oily fish; includes bream, flathead, whiting, snapper, dhufish, redfish and ling.

SHALLOTS also called french shallots, golden shallots or eschalots. Small and elongated, with a brown-skin, they grow in tight clusters similar to garlic.

SILVER BEET also called swiss chard and incorrectly, spinach; has fleshy stalks and large leaves, both of which can be prepared as for spinach.

SOUR CREAM a thick, commercially-cultured sour cream with a minimum fat content of 35 per cent.

SPINACH also called english spinach and, incorrectly, silver beet. Baby spinach leaves are best eaten raw in salads; the larger leaves should be added last to dishes, and cooked until barely wilted.

SUGAR
caster also called finely granulated or superfine sugar.
palm also called jaggery or gula melaka; made from the sap of the sugar palm tree. Light brown to dark-brown in colour and usually sold in rock-hard cakes. Substitute with brown sugar, if unavailable.
white coarse, granulated table sugar; also called crystal sugar.

TOMATO
canned whole peeled tomatoes in natural juices; available crushed, chopped or diced, and unsalted or reduced salt. Use undrained.
paste triple-concentrated tomato puree used to flavour soups, stews, sauces and casseroles.

VINEGAR
balsamic originally from Modena, Italy, there are now many balsamic vinegars on the market ranging in pungency and quality depending on how, and for how long, they have been aged. Quality can be determined up to a point by price; use the most expensive sparingly.
white made from distilled grain alcohol.

ZUCCHINI also called courgette.

CONVERSION CHART

MEASURES

One Australian metric measuring cup holds approximately 250ml, one Australian metric tablespoon holds 20ml, one Australian metric teaspoon holds 5ml.

The difference between one country's measuring cups and another's is within a 2- or 3-teaspoon variance, and will not affect your cooking results. North America, New Zealand and the United Kingdom use a 15ml tablespoon. All cup and spoon measurements are level. The most accurate way of measuring dry ingredients is to weigh them. When measuring liquids, use a clear glass or plastic jug with metric markings.

We use large eggs with an average weight of 60g.

DRY MEASURES

METRIC	IMPERIAL
15g	½oz
30g	1oz
60g	2oz
90g	3oz
125g	4oz (¼lb)
155g	5oz
185g	6oz
220g	7oz
250g	8oz (½lb)
280g	9oz
315g	10oz
345g	11oz
375g	12oz (¾lb)
410g	13oz
440g	14oz
470g	15oz
500g	16oz (1lb)
750g	24oz (1½lb)
1kg	32oz (2lb)

LIQUID MEASURES

METRIC	IMPERIAL
30ml	1 fluid oz
60ml	2 fluid oz
100ml	3 fluid oz
125ml	4 fluid oz
150ml	5 fluid oz
190ml	6 fluid oz
250ml	8 fluid oz
300ml	10 fluid oz
500ml	16 fluid oz
600ml	20 fluid oz
1000ml (1 litre)	32 fluid oz

LENGTH MEASURES

METRIC	IMPERIAL
3mm	⅛in
6mm	¼in
1cm	½in
2cm	¾in
2.5cm	1in
5cm	2in
6cm	2½in
8cm	3in
10cm	4in
13cm	5in
15cm	6in
18cm	7in
20cm	8in
23cm	9in
25cm	10in
28cm	11in
30cm	12in (1ft)

OVEN TEMPERATURES

The oven temperatures in this book are for conventional ovens; if you have a fan-forced oven, decrease the temperature by 10–20 degrees.

	°C (CELSIUS)	°F (FAHRENHEIT)
Very slow	120	250
Slow	150	300
Moderately slow	160	325
Moderate	180	350
Moderately hot	200	400
Hot	220	425
Very hot	240	475

INDEX

Reprinted in 2011 by Octopus Publishing Group Limited based on
materials licensed to it by ACP Magazines Ltd, a division of PBL Media Pty Limited

54 Park St, Sydney
GPO Box 4088, Sydney, NSW 2001
phone (02) 9282 8618; fax (02) 9267 9438
acpbooks@acpmagazines.com.au; www.acpbooks.com.au

ACP BOOKS

General manager Christine Whiston
Editor-in-chief Susan Tomnay
Creative director Hieu Chi Nguyen
Art director Hannah Blackmore
Designer Sarah Holmes
Senior editor Wendy Bryant
Food director Pamela Clark

Published and Distributed in the United Kingdom by Octopus Publishing Group Limited
Endeavour House
189 Shaftesbury Avenue
London WC2H 8JY
United Kingdom
phone + 44 (0) 207 632 5400; fax + 44 (0) 207 632 5405
aww@octopusbooks.co.uk; www.octopusbooks.co.uk
www.australian-womens-weekly.com

Printed and bound in China

A catalogue record for this book is available from the British Library.
ISBN 978-1-742450-18-6
First published by ACP Magazines Ltd in 2005

ABN 18 053 273 546

To order books:
telephone LBS on 01903 828 503
order online at www.australian-womens-weekly.com
or www.octopusbooks.co.uk

Send recipe enquiries to: recipeenquiries@acpmagazines.com.au